curious about

GRIFFINS

BY GINA KAMMER

AMICUS LEARNING

What are you

curious about?

CHAPTER THREE

3

Finding Griffins

PAGE

16

Curious About is published by
Amicus Learning, an imprint of Amicus
P.O. Box 227
Mankato, MN 56002
www.amicuspublishing.us

Editor: Ana Brauer
Series Designer: Kathleen Petelinsek
Book Designer: Kim Pfeffer
Photo Researchers: Katelynn Hope and Kim Pfeffer

Library of Congress Cataloging-in-Publication Data
Names: Kammer, Gina, author.
Title: Curious about griffins / by Gina Kammer.
Description: Mankato, MN : Amicus Learning, an imprint of Amicus, [2025] | Series: Curious about mythical creatures | Includes bibliographical references and index. | Audience: Ages 6–9 | Audience: Grades 2–3 | Summary: "What do griffins look like? Learn the Greek mythology concerning griffins in this question-and-answer book for elementary readers. Includes infographics, table of contents, glossary, books and websites for further research, and index"— Provided by publisher.
Identifiers: LCCN 2024017529 (print) | LCCN 2024017530 (ebook) | ISBN 9798892000987 (library binding) | ISBN 9798892001564 (paperback) | ISBN 9798892002141 (ebook)
Subjects: LCSH: Griffins—Miscellanea—Juvenile literature.
Classification: LCC BL325.G7 K36 2025 (print) | LCC BL325.G7 (ebook) | DDC 398.24/54—dc23/eng20240501
LC record available at https://lccn.loc.gov/2024017529
LC ebook record available at https://lccn.loc.gov/2024017530

Photo Credits: Adobe Stock/Dianne, 5, Hungarian, cover, Superhero Woozie, 14–15; Freepik/brain71, 13, Pikaso, 10–11, 16–17, 19, studioworkstock, 8, wirestock, 13; Shutterstock/Dominique de La Croix, 13, Sarunyu L, 20–21; Wikimedia Commons/Public Domain, 4, Wenceslaus Hollar, 7

Printed in China

CHAPTER ONE

What are griffins?

Griffins have appeared in art for thousands of years.

Guardians of gold! These legendary creatures are part eagle and part lion. They are **protectors**. But they also punish those who steal things. In Greek art, they pull gods' **chariots**. Sometimes gods ride them. Griffins are also called the "hounds of Zeus." Zeus is the king of the Greek gods.

Lions are the king of the jungle, and eagles are the king of the sky. This makes griffins especially powerful.

What do griffins look like?

Griffins have a lion's body. They have an eagle's head, wings, and claws. They are a little larger than a horse. Greeks thought there was another type of griffin in India that was smaller, like a wolf. They have black, red, and blue feathers. Their wings are white.

Greek griffins are the most common in modern art and stories.

DIFFERENT TYPES OF GRIFFINS

Are griffins real?

In myths, griffins symbolize strength and courage.

Not likely. But some people believed they might be real. Pictures go back at least 3,500 years. People told stories about griffins long before they wrote them down. The countries of Iran, Egypt, and Greece all have old griffin legends. But none have **proof** that they're real.

Griffins are found in different myths and stories around the world.

CHAPTER TWO

Griffins are fierce protectors.

What do griffins like to do?

Guard their gold—and eggs! They make nests with gold in them. They like shiny things. Don't try to steal from them! They don't like people who try to steal the gold. Plus, they're afraid you might hurt their chicks. Then they like to attack with their sharp claws and beaks.

What abilities do griffins have?

Guardian powers! Griffins can protect people and gold. They are strong and have powerful claws. Griffins can fight off **evil** or dark magic. They are brave and smart. Even their claws and eggs might be magical. People used them in **medicine** and as cups. They thought these would protect them from **poison**.

Legends say griffins have great eyesight. They can see gold from far away.

GRIFFINS EGGS AND CLAWS

People in the Middle Ages thought they found real griffin claws and eggs. But they were goat horns and ostrich eggs.

In stories, griffins typically stay away from humans. But they might protect a human who is trustworthy.

Are griffins friendly?

Maybe. Maybe not. Most griffins are wild. They fight to protect themselves. And they can beat both elephants and dragons in a fight. Griffins hate horses. In Greek myths, one-eyed horse riders tried to steal their gold. But some griffins serve kings and gods. Griffins guard them and fight for them.

CHAPTER THREE

Where do griffins live?

In myths, most griffins are found in northeastern Europe and central Asia. They live in groups. Griffins make nests on mountains near gold. They live away from people. Some might live in the flat grasslands. They make their nests on the ground.

In myths, griffins are very protective of their eggs and gold.

Could I fly on a griffin?

Are you a king? Or a god? Then maybe! But if not, don't try. A griffin might attack you! Or it might not carry you. A griffin has strong claws. But its wings aren't as powerful. It usually walks. But a griffin can fly for a short time. It flies fast!

COMPARING FLIGHT DISTANCE

Golden Eagle–125 miles (201.17 kilometers)

Griffin–20 miles (32.19 km)

Turkey–0.05 miles (0.08 km)

While the griffin has the wings of an eagle, it probably flies more like a turkey with its larger body—fast but for short distances only.

Griffins can fly at great heights and speeds. A human would have to hold on tight to ride one.

What else could a griffin be?

Protoceratops bones look like they could have belonged to a griffin.

It could be dinosaur bones! Traders found them in the Gobi Desert. One dinosaur's skull looks like a bird with a beak. These bones were near gold. So maybe people told stories to match. Or maybe people liked to imagine new creatures. They mixed animals together, just like they do today!

STAY CURIOUS!

ASK MORE QUESTIONS

What stories have people told about griffins?

What can I find out from old griffin pictures?

Try a BIG QUESTION: Where can I see griffins today?

SEARCH FOR ANSWERS

Search the library catalog or the Internet.
A librarian, teacher, or parent can help you.

Using Keywords
Find the looking glass.

Keywords are the most important words in your question.

If you want to know about:

- Griffin stories, type: GRIFFIN MYTHS
- Griffins in pictures, type: GRIFFINS IN ANCIENT ART

LEARN MORE

FIND GOOD SOURCES

Are the sources reliable?
Some sources are better than others. An adult can help you. Here are some good, safe sources.

Books

A First Look at Monsters
by Emma Carlson Berne, 2021.

Griffins
by Matt Doeden, 2020.

Internet Sites

Kiddle: Griffin Facts for Kids
https://kids.kiddle.co/Griffin
Kiddle is an encyclopedia for kids with facts on many topics.

Wonderopolis: What Is a Griffin?
https://wonderopolis.org/wonder/what-is-a-griffin
Wonderopolis is created by The National Center for Families Learning, which provides resources for families.

SHARE AND TAKE ACTION

Where can you see griffins today?
Ask an adult to help you look for statues and logos on buildings or online.

What makes nests on mountains?
Find out which creatures might live in places griffins like.

Make up your own creature!
Mix two animals together and draw its picture. Share your choices with family and friends.

GLOSSARY

chariot A two-wheeled carriage usually pulled by horses.

evil Something or someone bad or cruel; wanting to hurt others.

medicine Something used to heal or treat sickness or pain.

poison Something that can kill or hurt people or animals when they swallow it.

proof Facts or evidence that show something is true.

protector One who keeps someone or something safe.

INDEX

About the Author

Gina Kammer grew up writing and illustrating her own stories. Now she teaches others to write stories at inkybookwyrm.com. She likes reading fantasy and medieval literature. She also enjoys traveling, oil painting, archery, and snuggling her grumpy bunny. She lives in Minnesota.